PILL$ AND BILL$

How to Lose It All
and End Up in a Nursing Home!

The Complete Guide to Extreme Poverty

Robert L. Cochran, LTCP, CLU, ChFC, RHU

NARROW WAY PUBLISHING™

Narrow Way Publishing, LLC
3878 N. Lake Orlando Parkway
Orlando, FL 32808

ISBN: 978-0-615-19167-6

www.PillsandBills.com

This book is dedicated to the love of my life, my beautiful wife, Saneen. You have always been my hero and even after all these years, you are still the finest person I have ever known. Loving you is the greatest privilege of my life and if the time comes that you are in need of care, it will be my honor and privilege to take care of and protect you.

Contents

Preface

Pills and Bills is born out of my personal experiences in working with hundreds of people over a period of many years. These experiences have convinced me beyond any doubt that people are in desperate need of the information contained in this book. There is a crisis occurring in families all across this country and much of the time it is self-induced and could have been completely avoided if only they would have had the proper knowledge. That is the aim of this book.

Pills and Bills is a metaphor for that inevitable stage of life when managing our medications and handling the expenses related to our health care requires more of our time and attention than ever before. I am looking forward to our time together and hope that you will learn and benefit from the experiences of the many people I have met along the way.

I have written this book in a satirical way in order to make it more interesting and in a conversational style to be more casual and informal. I have intentionally made it as brief as possible because I know that your time is valuable. So, get comfortable in your favorite spot and let's spend a few minutes together.

Introduction

How to lose it all and end up in a nursing home is really a very simple process and I promise that this book will show you how to accomplish it. Don't be discouraged, anyone can do it. In fact, I will venture to say that you are probably well on your way and a lot further along in the process than you are giving yourself credit for. The reason is that you naturally and instinctively have everything you need to make this a reality. All you need to do is to follow your instincts, seek advice from friends and family, read articles, and talk to experts in the wrong fields.

In fact, I can save you a tremendous amount of time along your journey through this process of *losing it all and ending up in a nursing home* because each chapter in this book will provide you with the exact same information you will get from each of these sources. The good news is that you do not have to adopt or accept each and every one of these beliefs that are presented as individual chapters in order to accomplish your goal. It is even simpler than that. If you can convince yourself to accept and believe *just one of them*, then that should do the trick and you will be well on your way to *losing it all and ending up in a nursing home.* So, pick whichever one you like best and makes you feel the most comfortable.

They all work pretty much the same when it comes to accomplishing your goal.

I should tell you that I could have entitled this book "Why I *don't* need long-term care insurance," but I didn't think that would capture your attention and cause you to take advantage of this very important material. So, let's have some fun as I share this helpful and important information with you, but do so in a way that hopefully, will be entertaining and keep your attention.

Now, there is only one thing that I need for you to bring along on our journey and that is your MIND. If you are the type of person who believes in fairy tales and thinks that if you hope that something will be a certain way it will, then this book probably isn't going to help you very much. But, if you are willing to be intellectually honest with yourself and use your powers of logic and reason, then you will benefit greatly from this book.

So, let's begin our exciting journey toward losing it all and ending up in extreme poverty.

Chapter 1
I Don't Think It Will Happen to Me

I know that if you are of even reasonable intelligence, this statement is hard to say with a straight face and make yourself believe, but try, because if you can, this is one of the best ways to ensure that you could *lose it all and end up in a nursing home.* And, you know what? I am betting that you can do it because I have talked to hundreds of people just like you who have said *I don't think it will happen to me* and, always with a straight face. If they can do it, you can, too! You see, pretending that it won't happen and sticking your head in the sand works really well. It is something we all learned when we were kids growing up. Remember, you just covered your ears with both hands and started mumbling something like la, la, la, la, la, whenever someone was telling you something you didn't want to hear? It usually worked pretty well, didn't it?

Now, for heaven's sake, whatever you do, don't let yourself be even remotely concerned with the following information or you could mess things up big time and NOT *lose it all and end up in a nursing home.* For example, do not believe that any of the following conditions that often cause the need for long-term care will ever happen to you and/or your spouse, if married: *Spinal cord injuries, stroke, physical frailty, Alzheimer's disease, Huntington's disease, dementia, senility, AIDS, Diabetes, autoimmune disorders such as Rheumatoid arthritis or Lupus, circulatory diseases and heart conditions, Parkinson's disease, Lou Gehrig's disease and multiple sclerosis among others.*

It would also be quite helpful to our cause of *losing it all and ending up in a nursing home* if you could find *some* way, *any* way, to dismiss the following information:

The Alzheimer's Association recently reported that the prevalence of Alzheimer's disease has increased 10 percent in the last five years and that someone in America develops Alzheimer's every 72 seconds.[1]

In 2005, about 10 million people age 18 or older needed assistance from others to perform everyday activities, and more than 30 million had some type of activity limitation.[2]

Over the next 15 years, the number of people who need long-term care is expected to increase by 30 percent. Soon thereafter, the number of people likely to need long-term care is expected to increase even more dramatically. Estimates of the long-term care population suggest that the number of people with long-term care needs will more than double between 2000 and 2050.[3]

Everyone is at risk not only of having a family member in need of long term care, but also of needing assistance themselves. About 45 percent of the long term care population is under the age of 65. Yet although the need for health insurance to cover a patient's medical expenses in case of catastrophic illness is widely recognized, few people are insured against the costs of providing long term support services for that same person. This lack of insurance coverage jeopardizes the financial security of families and diminishes the economic security of the country.[4]

Now, if your intellect is causing you a problem and making it really difficult for you to dismiss these statistics, then do the next best thing and just cover your ears and start mumbling something, anything to drown out this information while telling yourself that *you are lucky*, so it probably won't happen to you.

And, don't worry about those people who will try to confuse you with their logic and reason. They just don't "get it." They will tell you that doing nothing to protect yourself because you don't think it will happen to you makes about as much sense as saying, "I don't believe that my home will get broken into tonight, so I don't need to worry about locking my doors and turning on the alarm." Or, "I don't think my home will burn down, so who needs fire insurance." Don't listen to them; you must remember that they are just trying to stand in the way of us reaching our goals.

You just stick to your guns and keep saying over and over again to yourself, "I don't think it will happen to me, I don't think it will happen to me." If you say it enough, you have a good chance of making yourself believe it, and you'll be in a much better position to *lose it all and end up in a nursing home.*

Chapter 2
The Government Will Take Care of Me

This is a great one to adopt and believe because you have size on your side. You have the Federal Government—the massive, mammoth Federal Government, red, white and blue, for the people, the whole nine yards—on your side. Plus, you have the added benefit of having three different, very large government programs that you can lump together for added comfort. For example, try saying something like this: "I'm not worried about it, because Social Security, Medicare, or Medicaid (one of these programs, I'm just not sure which one) will take care of me." Now, take a deep breath and say "Ahh!" Don't you feel nice and comfy? Now, if you can, try and leave it real broad and general like that. Make sure that you do not get too specific and try to understand what each of them actually does, or you might get concerned and that would mess everything up.

In other words, it is much easier if you can lump them all together and draw comfort from the fact that of the three large government programs, surely one of them will take care of you. After all, isn't that why you pay taxes? Do not let yourself be tempted to separate the three of them and actually learn what they do because that information could be devastating to the fulfillment of your plan. It might cause you to take matters into your own hands and plan for the future and that could jeopardize you *losing it all and ending up in a nursing home*. For example:

It would behoove you *not* to know that *Social Security* has absolutely nothing to do with long term care. That the primary function and purpose of Social Security is to pay you a retirement check in return for the years that both you and the employers you worked for paid Social Security taxes into the system. Or, that *Medicare* doesn't pay for long-term care, but rather only short-term care up to approximately three months and only if you continue to meet a number of requirements that most people don't. Therefore, the average length of time they pay is usually much less than that. Or, that *Medicaid* is a welfare program for the poor that only pays after you have first spent almost all of your life savings on your own care. And then, you become a ward of the state and lose many of your options and control over the type of care you receive and where it is provided.

But listen, if you are starting to falter or waiver, quickly grab hold of this lifeline and maybe you can hang on a little longer to your belief that the government will take care of you. I know this is hard, but you can do it! I would suggest using a diversionary tactic and tell yourself something like this, "Well, you know what? By the time I need this kind of care I will be so bad off and so out of it that I won't even know what is going on anyway." But here's a tip: make sure you don't go to a nursing home and observe all of the people there who *are* in their right minds and *do know* exactly what is going on. But, if that should happen, try to get your mind off it as quickly as possible and immediately go back to comforting yourself with the notion that surely the government is going to step in and take care of not only you, but everyone else as well.

If you will just continue telling yourself that, I am confident that in no time you will be right back on track to *losing it all and ending up in a nursing home.*

Chapter 3
My Children Will Take Care of Me

Now, you have every right to believe and expect that your problems, burdens, and misfortunes should become the curse and scourge of the ones you love most. This is truly the gift that keeps on giving. And, you know what? It won't even get old with them. They will be just as excited and happy to do it after the first year or two as they were after the first week. Actually, this is every child's dream; we all anxiously anticipate getting to be our parent's primary care givers. And we are not even uncomfortable seeing our parents naked as we bathe them or change their diapers. When your kids tell you that it is no problem and they are happy to do it, you just believe them. Don't even let your mind wonder about how they will really feel or what they will be saying behind closed doors after they have finally tucked you in for the night and have collapsed into bed. After all, they will probably be saying that they can't wait until tomorrow when they get to do it all over again.

Whatever you do, do not focus or think about the toll it will take on them or their families. After all, isn't it every parent's right to ruin their children's lives? Besides, you can bet that they will sing your praises to all of their friends for not planning ahead and being too cheap to buy that insurance that would have paid for other people to help them care for you and given everybody a better quality of life. And don't worry, it probably won't cross their minds that when they naively and lovingly said that they would always take care of you, that it gave you just the out you were looking for. After all, they knew what they were getting into when they said that, and most certainly wouldn't have had it any other way. So, put those thoughts of you being selfish, a burden, and a home wrecker right out of your mind.

Also, don't worry about having to relocate across the country and leaving your home with its memories and all of your friends behind. The change of scenery will do you good. Who wouldn't jump at the chance to spend the remaining years of their life in a strange city or town? If anyone tries to convince you that this is not a perfect plan by sharing real life stories with you like the following that a friend shared with me, you just ignore them. After all, I am sure that it is isolated to his family and things like this do not happen to other families. So, fret not, just enjoy it and be glad that nothing like this could ever happen to you.

My friend's mother was aging and having some medical problems that required her to need care. She had not planned ahead, so there was no well thought-out plan created in the absence of crisis. Therefore, my friend, who was married and had a young child, decided that the only thing they could do was to move his Mom from her home state to the where they lived. Well, that created a problem because their home was not large enough for all of them, so they decided to go out on a limb and buy a larger home (more expensive than they could really afford) that would provide enough room for all of them to live comfortably. They moved Mom in, but she did not adjust too well to moving to a new area and having everything in her life change. But, that wasn't all, my friend and his wife were not used to someone else telling them how to raise their child and criticizing everything they did. After a number of disagreements and heated discussions, Mom had all the fun she could take, packed up, and skipped town in the middle of the night to go back home. Relationships were torn and damaged, lifestyles were forever altered, and they were right back where they started with the exact same problem—Mom was still aging and having medical problems that required her to need care, and they were no closer to any solutions.

But listen, I am concerned that you could get swayed by this story, so let me give you a little something that will help you stay strong. Just repeat after me. "It's all about me, it's all about me, it's all about me." Whenever you feel a weak moment coming on and genuine love and concern for your family trying to creep in, just repeat this over and over again until that awful feeling has passed. Once it has passed, and it will, just go back to telling yourself how great it is going to be having the family together again, just like old times, and how much *fun* the kids are going to have taking care of you.

Chapter 4
It's Too Expensive, I Can't Afford It

Now, this is about the smartest one yet, because it stops those who are against us dead in their tracks. Who can argue with this one? I already have to pay for my pills and all my other bills, how can I afford to pay for anything else? It carries with it the air of us being so intelligent and wise when it comes to how we handle money. Besides, this is the same standard that we always apply to every area of our spending, right? It's not like we're just using it as a convenient excuse because we don't want to spend money to take responsibility for ourselves. Actually, don't tell anyone, but it is kind of convenient that we have this one at our disposal to use whenever and however we need it. How we chose to use it is nobody else's business. And after all, isn't it a beautiful thing that we have suddenly "seen the light" when it comes to handling money wisely? Don't you worry about any apparent inconsistencies between your newfound financial high road when it comes to this issue and how you handle money in other areas of your life. If anyone tries to call you on it, let me recommend using any of the following excuses—they are tried and true and have stood the test of time. Just tell them that you have "seen the errors of your ways," "learned from your past mistakes," "turned over a new leaf," or that "it is never too late to start over." Any one of these, or even stringing them all together for added effect, should work just fine.

What is so brilliant about this one is that it allows you to appear to be so concerned about the issue without actually having to take any responsibility for it. "If I could afford to buy insurance to protect myself, I certainly would, but I just can't, so there's nothing I can do about it." Presto, you're off the hook! This one is about as good as it gets; however, I do need to let you know that even with this one there are a few risks that you need to be aware of so that you are not caught off guard. For example:

It would be helpful if, once you have gotten to this point, you quickly file it away and try not to revisit the subject again. The reason is that you probably had to be a little dishonest to convince yourself that it was too expensive and that you couldn't afford it. If you don't leave this one alone as quickly as possible, you might find yourself asking questions that are totally counterproductive to our goal of *losing it all and ending up in a nursing home*. In a moment of doubt, you could be tempted to ask questions such as: too expensive compared to what? Or, is it that I really can't afford it or just that I would rather spend my money on other things and it is not a priority? Ouch, see what I mean? You really need to steer clear of letting yourself go there, because if that were true, then it would almost surely imply that you were just being irresponsible. The beauty of this one is that it gives you the illusion of being responsible without having to accept any responsibility. And that, my friend, is brilliant. Pure genius. To be able to pull that off, you deserve much kudos for a well done self-deception. So, just leave well enough alone or you may ruin everything by letting unproductive questions and doubts enter your mind. I'm telling you, it is a no win situation. Can you imagine having to answer such questions as: If I can't afford to pay for insurance, which only costs a fraction of the actual cost of receiving care, how in the world could I afford to pay for the care itself? Or, if I really can afford to buy the insurance, but just don't want to spend the money, how will I feel about having to spend more money in just one month to pay for my care than I would have spent in an entire year for the insurance? Plus, what if this continues year after year for many years? How will I be able to afford that?

Wow, at this point I think you need to immediately go to other chapters in this book for additional reinforcement. Although holding on to just one of our core beliefs will normally be sufficient to do the job, occasionally you may need a short-term fix to get you over the hump. Without added support, I am concerned that you might be overcome by our arch enemy, logic and reason, and end up squandering your opportunity to *lose it all and end up in a nursing home.* May I be so bold as to suggest belief number 1, *I don't think it will happen to me,* or maybe even number 5, which we will discuss next, *I will just take my chances?* Incorporating both of them should be extremely helpful. Actually, at such a critical juncture, adding any one or more of our core beliefs should bring the needed comfort and relief. And, don't worry; this should only be a temporary situation. Once you get things under control, you should be able to scale back to just your original belief: *It's too expensive, I can't afford it.*

Now, when it comes time to write those large monthly checks as you go through the process of *losing it all on your way to the nursing home*, you should find great comfort in reminding yourself that you couldn't afford the insurance because it was just too expensive.

Chapter 5
I'm Just Going to Take My Chances

Whenever I hear someone say, "I'll just take my chances," I get very concerned about that person's commitment to our program of *losing it all and ending up in a nursing home.* The reason is that they are not in nearly as much denial as the person who says *I don't think it will happen to me.* And this is very disturbing because we are in great peril of losing them to the other side. You see, they have already started to buy into the lie that maybe it could happen to them, and they are barely holding on by a thread. They have moved to the center by admitting that it *could* happen to them, but they'll just take their chances. Do you see it? It is right there and it is so subtle and dangerous. They have moved from I *don't think* it will happen to me to it *could* happen to me. Folks, that is a huge acknowledgement and now all they are hanging onto is *but* I'll just take my chances. Do you realize how vulnerable they are to being picked off by the other side when some smooth talking person comes along and starts whispering sweet something's in their ear? Sweet something's like the following:

More than half of the U.S. population will require long term care at some point in their lives.[5]

60% of Americans who reach age 65 will need long-term care at some point in their lives.[6]

The lifetime probability of becoming disabled in at least two activities of daily living or of being cognitively impaired is 68% for people age 65 and older.[7]

One out of five Americans over the age of 50 is at risk of needing long term care in the next 12 months.[8]

40% of those receiving long-term care are working-age adults, ages 18-64, due to accidents, strokes, brain injuries or tumors, mental conditions, AIDS, multiple sclerosis, muscular dystrophy, and even early onset of Alzheimer's and Parkinson's disease.[9]

The U.S. Department of Health and Human Services reports that the total number of Americans needing long-term care is expected to rise from 15 million in 2000 to 27 million in 2050, an increase of nearly 100%.[10]

We must encourage our followers to hold firm and not be seduced by these sweet somethings. They may even use the clincher, which will be to ask, since you are just going to take your chances, don't you think it would be wise to know your chances of *losing*? Well, not to worry, it really doesn't matter because **losing it all and ending up in a nursing home** is our goal. So, either way we win!

Chapter 6
I'm Never Going to a Nursing Home

This one is universal, and therefore, one of our most effective weapons. Because we know that everyone feels strongly about never going to a nursing home, we can actually turn the tables and use this very thing to *accomplish* our goal of *losing it all and ending up in a nursing home.* See, if you will just avoid discussing this issue and purchasing insurance to protect yourself because your mind is made up that you are never going to a nursing home, then you have actually just *increased the odds* of that very thing occurring.

You know the old saying, "talk is cheap." You can talk all you want about how you're never going to a nursing home, and as long as all you do is talk about it and make sure that you never take any action to prevent it, then you are right where you need to be. The beauty of this one is that the nursing homes are full of people who swore that *they* would never go to a nursing home. So, this strategy obviously works. It was their lack of planning that helped cause them to end up in a place where they said they never wanted to go. Therefore, one of the best ways to *lose it it all and end up in a nursing home* is to convince yourself that you don't need to worry about long-term care insurance because you are never going to a nursing home. Do you get it?

Now, of course, the enemy—the other side—will again use logic and reason to try and trip you up. They always do. You must never forget that all they care about is the accomplishment of their own agenda, which is to *keep you from losing it all and ending up in a nursing home.* They want to create doubt in your mind so that you will do something foolish like protecting yourself and your family. And they will use any means to accomplish their goal. They will even stoop so low as to point out the following statistics which show that the majority of care people receive occurs at home and in the community, *not in nursing homes.*

> *Most people—nearly 79%—who need long-term care live at home or in community settings, not in institutions.[11]*

> *More than four-fifths (83%) of people with long-term care needs live in the community.[12]*

They are very cunning and will do anything to have you know the truth, which is that in addition to nursing homes, long-term care insurance *also* covers care at *home* and in the *community.* They are well aware that if you know this, you might figure out that owning this kind of insurance could actually keep you from *losing it all and ending up in a nursing home* by paying for you to stay in your *own home* and receive care.

But, don't you fall for any of this. Why in the world would you want to stay at home and keep your money when you could *lose it all and end up in a nursing home?* You just recommit 100% to telling yourself that you don't need to worry about any of this because you are never going to a nursing home.

Chapter 7
I Am Going to Do Something,
Just Not Right Now

Of course you are. You have every intention of addressing this issue and you'll get around to it one day. There is no hurry, why rush? The important thing is that you are *planning* on doing it, not that you actually ever *do* it. In fact, if you ever did do it instead of just talking about it, you could really sabotage everything. It could all backfire and cause you to NOT lose it all and NOT end up in a nursing home. And, if that were to happen, you would have absolutely no one to blame but yourself, so don't come crying to me. I am trying to share everything I have learned, all of the very best ideas out there for how to *lose it all and end up in a nursing home.* If you chose to ignore everything that I am sharing with you and go ahead and take action to prevent it from happening, then shame on you. As far as I am concerned, you will deserve whatever you get, and if it costs you your opportunity to *blow it all and end up in a nursing home,* then so be it. You will just have to sleep in the bed that you made even if it's not in a nursing home for poor people.

I am so sorry. I have no idea what got into me. I don't know why I came down so hard on you, you certainly didn't deserve that. After all, you have never given even the slightest indication that you would act on what you are saying and it wasn't right for me to judge you like that. I guess I just get a little paranoid because I know how relentless our enemy, "the truth," can be sometimes and I don't want to see you give up when you have come so far. I want you to know that I really do empathize with you because I know it isn't always easy to keep convincing yourself of some of our beliefs. But, it is worth it because I promise you, they work. And, you have to admit they sure do make you feel good along the way, don't they?

Anyway, back to the point. *I am going to do something, just not right now* is one of my favorites because it is so easy to make yourself believe it. And, as long as you believe that one day you'll get to it, you can relax and not worry about a thing. It should make you feel nice and warm, safe and secure, just like being draped under your favorite binky. The rest will pretty much take care of itself, because using this one is almost a guaranteed fail-proof way of assuring that you *lose it all and end up in a nursing home*. The reason is that even though you really want to do something (wink, wink) you are just waiting for the right time. And, that elusive "right time" part is our out. Don't you see it? It never comes and it never will. Life, combined with your powers of denial, delusion, and procrastination, will make sure of that and it will be no time at all before you will have lost it all and are making wonderful new friends at Shady Oaks.

So, keep the faith and press on!

Chapter 8
I'm Just Going to Self-Insure
(a.k.a. How to Run with the Big Dogs
and Get Eaten Alive)

Since everybody knows that it's the insurance companies that have all the money, why not just be your own insurance company, you big dog you! Just think how much money you would save if you paid yourself the premiums for all the different insurance policies that you have. My goodness, in no time you could be wealthy enough to self-insure everything. Oh, but wait a second, you're supposed to already be wealthy enough to self-insure before you actually do it. Well, you know what, don't worry about that minor detail. So what if you can't really afford to do it, neither can most of the other people who are using this one; you will be in good company, my friend. By now you should know the drill anyway. It's not about whether you can really afford it, it's about whether it makes you feel like a big dog and gets you out of having to spend money on something that you don't want to spend it on. Remember, the only thing that matters is that we *lose it all and end up in a nursing home*. How we get there doesn't matter. If this one feels good to you, then just adopt it, believe it, and you'll be half way home to the nursing home.

The beauty behind this one is that few people ever go to the trouble of actually figuring out whether they can afford to self-insure or not. In fact, it's essential that you don't either if you want to use this one to your full advantage. You must resist the temptation to do any mathematical calculations, or you can kiss this one good-bye. Now, I am not worried about the temptation coming from within, because we aren't going to be foolish enough to blow our own cover, we have way too much denial already invested. As always, the threat will come from the other side, so we must never let our guard down. We must always remember that they don't have our best interest at heart. All they want to do is take a little of our money to ensure that we don't *lose it all and end up in a nursing home.* How appalling and offensive! They have absolutely no concern for us or the things that are important to us. How foolish do they think we are? If it were up to them, we would all keep our money and age in dignity and grace at home with our families. Hello people, do you really think they care about you? Wake up!

If you are going to protect yourself against the enemy, then you must know how they are going to attack you. And attack you they will. As you might expect by now, their main weapon is going to be logic and reason. They keep coming at us with the same old strategy. They certainly aren't a very creative bunch. You would think they would use smoke and mirrors, bells and whistles or something, but no, they just keep pounding away with logic and reason. They will tell you that you might want to first start your self-insuring plan with the items that have much less value and much less chance of occurring like canceling your car insurance, homeowners insurance, jewelry insurance, etc. Their logic will be that it would be foolish to pay the insurance company to insure the cheaper things that have less chance of something happening to them while you cover the things that are at much greater risk and could be much more financially devastating. They will try to take you back to insurance 101—the first insurance class they ever attended. This is where they learned that the most basic premise behind the concept of insurance is to transfer the catastrophic risks (big ones) to someone else with deeper pockets than your own. Why assume a risk that could wipe you out when, for a fraction of the cost, you could transfer the risk to someone else who can afford to handle the loss much better?

Then they will really try to mess you up by pointing out that with all this talk about self-insuring, even very few of the truly wealthy people ever go without auto or homeowners insurance. In fact, usually the wealthier the person is, the more insurance they have. They usually own umbrella policies that cover them for millions of dollars over and above their regular auto and homeowner's insurance policies in case they ever get sued. And, on a percentage basis, how often do you think that happens? So, if it isn't the very wealthy who are doing all of this self-insuring, then who is it? Unfortunately, it is the less wealthy who are kidding themselves and using this as an excuse to not spend money for protection against the risk of needing long-term care. The truth is that the very people who are talking about self-insuring are usually the ones who can least afford it. The only reason that they are considering it is because they don't even want to spend the relatively small amount of money that the insurance would cost. That being the case, how will they feel about spending the large amounts of money required to pay for their own care? Does this sound like the kind of big dog that can afford to self-insure much of anything?

Now, if you are dealing with someone from the other side who is honest, you will be able to get them to admit that some people really are so wealthy that they could afford to self-insure themselves against the risk of needing long-term care. They will admit that in good conscience there is no way they would even attempt to convince these people that they *need* to have long-term care insurance. What they will tell you, however, is that many of these same people decide that even though they may not *need* long-term care insurance, they actually *want* it. While that may surprise you because you seem to think that the whole goal is to self-insure in order to avoid paying for insurance, you have to remember that these are some of the smartest people in society who have achieved great wealth. They did not get there by being foolish with how they handle their finances. They understand that if they could truly afford to spend $130,000 - $150,000 per year for 24-hour round the clock care at home (which you can bet is the only place that they have any interest in staying) and never bat an eye, then why in the world wouldn't they spend a fraction of that for insurance and never bat an eye. That way they get to keep all that they have accumulated and use it in the ways that are most important to them. It may be their children, their church, or many other worthwhile charities. This is the same reason that they spend thousands of dollars to do estate planning in order to minimize their taxes as much as possible and make sure that their money goes where they ultimately desire it to go. Sure, they could afford to pay the taxes, but they would prefer not to if they can avoid it. There's no difference. This is also why they still carry insurance on their cars, homes, and other personal effects. They would rather someone else incur the financial loss than themselves. Remember, these are savvy people when it comes to financial matters. They did not become wealthy by being foolish with the way they handle their finances.

So, be prepared. They are going to come at you with exactly this kind of reasoning. If you ever drop your guard and even start to contemplate accepting logic, reason, and commonsense, then you are dead in the water, game over. We must accept the fact that we can never compete against them on these terms and win. But, not to worry, if we just stick to our guns and keep using our primary defense, which, of course, is denial, there is nothing they can say or do to thwart our efforts to *lose it all and end up in a nursing home.*

So, stay the course, my friend. Your destination is in sight.

Chapter 9
I Read an Article That Said
I Should Wait Until Age ??
to Buy Long-Term Care Insurance

This one is similar to belief number 7, but has the added benefit of having your procrastination blessed by a "so-called" expert. It doesn't get much better than that. The official diagnosis is "Expert Sanctioned Procrastination Syndrome," commonly known as ESPS. The good news is that it is extremely contagious and once a person is inflicted with this insidious disease, they almost never recover from it. The reason is that it attacks the part of the brain where logic and reason occur. Of all of the cases of ESPS that I have treated over the years, I am pleased to report that the effects are almost always irreversible. I have rarely ever seen anyone recover from this condition. There was one case that was an anomaly, which I will share in a moment; however, it is so rare that you don't need to be too concerned about it.

My theory for the low recovery rate of ESPS is that the pedestal that the so-called expert sits on is perceived to be so high and the message being delivered so appealing to the senses, that the combination of the two creates a chemical reaction that goes directly to the part of the brain where denial and procrastination lie dormant.

Once this chemical comes in contact with the denial and procrastination that is stored there, it starts a chemical reaction, which essentially has the effect of causing one to lose all ability to think rationally for oneself and puts them at the mercy of the so-called expert. If the so-called expert says to wait until a certain age to consider protecting themselves with long-term care insurance, then they willingly comply by intending to procrastinate until the suggested age. This is a very exciting and promising development in the field of poverty because, as we have already learned, procrastination is one of our best friends when it comes to *losing it all and ending up in a nursing home.* Just imagine the good that could be done for the redistribution of wealth in this country (your wealth) and the unemployment rate in the nursing home industry. This is what we call a triple win. You win because you accomplish your goal of *losing it all and ending up in a nursing home,* society wins because your wealth is redistributed into the system, and the unemployment rate is reduced in the nursing home sector due to increased demand for services.

Where this exciting development falls short, however, is the fact that the subject is actually encouraged to buy long-term care insurance at some point in the future. Obviously, if they were to follow through on this recommendation, many of them would never qualify for coverage at that point due to changes in their health, so we don't have to worry about them. It's the remaining ones we need to be worried about. While it's true that they would be paying a much higher premium due to their older age, in addition to any premium increases that the insurance company had incurred, nonetheless if they took the so-called expert's advice and purchased coverage, they would still be protected. This could be devastating to our mission and would jeopardize the fulfillment of our goal of *losing it all and ending up in a nursing home.*

Not to worry though. We have several aces in the hole, which will come to our rescue. First off, as I mentioned, many of them will have shot themselves in the foot by following the advice of the so-called expert which was to put off purchasing insurance until they reached a certain age. At that point, they won't be healthy enough to buy this kind of insurance for all the money in the world. That you can take to the bank. So, that eliminates them. Secondly, if they didn't want to spend the money when they were younger and it was a lot less expensive, do you really think they are going to be willing to spend it now when the cost is so much higher? No way, baby! They are going to revert back to number 4 and say that *it is too expensive and they can't afford it.* Trust me; I've seen it happen a million times. It's like fool's gold. They have fooled themselves into thinking they've got something (a plan), but in reality they just end up with nothing, no plan at all. They are right back where they started. They really think they will deal with this down the road, but it's just an illusion, a mirage. When they get there, they realize that the same reasons they weren't willing to deal with it sooner are still there, only bigger now.

Now, in the spirit of full disclosure, I do need to let you know that occasionally this condition can be reversed. I treated a person with ESPS once who, in spite of the odds, did recover and went on to fail miserably by protecting herself with long-term care insurance. She had received the advice of a so-called expert who, when she asked about long-term care insurance, told her that she was too young and didn't need to worry about it for quite some time. Since she was obviously dealing with someone who had the ability to read the future, she should have asked him which stock to invest in, in which case she could have bought the nursing home and been done with it. Anyway, what caused her to recover was her uncontrollable ability to think for herself. That may have something to do with the fact that she was very intelligent. She was a Certified Public Accountant who had her own practice. When this so-called expert gave her that advice, she said that after thinking about it for a minute she asked him, "But what if something has happened to my health and I am not able to get the coverage then?" She said that he looked at her kind of perplexed and said, "Well you have a point there; that could be a problem."

Well, like I said earlier, I really wouldn't worry about this happening because it is so rare. I have a professional responsibility to tell you about it, but you certainly don't need to lose any sleep over it. We're not going to win them all, but trust me, we are winning much more than our fair share and the above advice from so-called experts is one of the main reasons why we are able to help so many people *lose it all and end up in a nursing home.*

Chapter 10
There Is Longevity in My Family, So I Don't Need to Worry About It

Makes sense to me! If everybody in your family lives a long time, then why ever worry about needing *long-term* care? Anything that would happen to you would probably just be short-term in nature. Huh? Don't worry about the logic here. It works for our purposes and that is all that matters. As long as it moves us closer toward our goal of *losing it all and ending up in a nursing home*, it's all good. Remember, it doesn't really matter how sound it is, what matters is how soundly you can sleep by believing it. And, this one works for many people. So, don't discount its power no matter how illogical it seems. As shallow as it may appear, I must tell you I have seen many people use it effectively to accomplish their goal.

The only area where this one leaves you vulnerable is from those bubble bursters who will try and stir up trouble. They will suggest that those with longevity in their family may very well hang on and need care much longer than those with inferior blood lines. Don't buy into their theory that in many cases longevity might actually be a negative thing. It is a very alarming theory that suggests that living longer may not necessarily mean living better. Its premise is that with the advances in medical technology, combined with good heredity, and people being more health conscious, they are likely to live much longer and require more care than their feeble friends.

I hope you understand why I am concerned. This is very discouraging and a direct challenge to the false sense of security that you normally expect to be associated with this particular belief. Nevertheless, all is not lost. I have still seen many people enjoy great success using this one. Besides, you have many other options at your disposal should you find this one no longer serving its purpose. Remember, any goal that is worth accomplishing is worth working for. I promised that this book would show you how to *lose it all and end up in a nursing home*, but you have to be willing to do your part.

Can I still count on you?

Chapter 11
If I Wait and Buy Later, I'll Save Money

This one is the brother of *I am going to do something, just not right now*. In another chapter we discussed ESPS—Expert Sanctioned Procrastination Syndrome—but, for you do-it-yourselfers who don't need the approval and affirmation of an expert in order to feel comfortable procrastinating, let me suggest taking a nice little cruise aboard the SS LIPS. The SS LIPS stands for Self-Sanctioned Logic-Induced Procrastination Syndrome. With this one, you electric slide yourself right into the ole' nursing home after losing it all at the black jack table of life. You'll be the life of the party and the envy of all as you sail across the dance floor while performing each move of your poverty polka with precision and grace.

The beauty of this one is that it lets you feel like you are prudently addressing the issue by making a decision to do something, but just later since it will save you money. Hard to argue with logic like that, isn't it? Saving money is never a bad thing. Oh, and don't think that I missed how you turned the tables and used a little logic of your own to work things to your advantage by postponing having to deal with this issue until down the road. Quite brilliant! Logic and reason has long been our enemy's number one weapon for trying to keep us from *losing it all and ending up in a nursing home* and now you have found a way to make it your justification for accomplishing exactly that. It doesn't get any better than that! Anyway, because this one is so obvious and logical, you don't need anyone else to bless it or give you permission to procrastinate. You'll gladly accept full responsibility for this one on your own, thus, the name Self-Sanctioned Logic-Induced Procrastination Syndrome.

Now, don't worry if you aren't quite sure how waiting to buy coverage until later will translate into accomplishing your goal of *losing it all and ending up in a nursing home*. I am happy to explain. It really wouldn't if you were to actually follow through on buying the coverage later, but since there's very little chance of that happening, you don't need to worry about it. You see, your ability to procrastinate is what will save the day. You will procrastinate and procrastinate and procrastinate until one day either your health will have changed and purchasing coverage is no longer an option, or the cost will be so high that you won't be able to bring yourself to spend the money. Either way, your powers of denial will kick in like endorphins and you will convince yourself that even though all of your options are gone, it's no big deal because you never really wanted the protection and nothing is ever going to happen to you anyway.

You see, changes in health will get a bunch of folks, and when the rest find out how costly the insurance has become by then, they will quickly realize that their belief that they were going to save money by waiting was flawed right from the get go. Someone from the other side will be more than happy to point out that you don't have to be a Phi Beta Kappa from MIT to figure out the math. They will show you that, for example, if the cost of care is currently $6,000 per month in your area and that cost increases by 5% per year, then in 10 years, when you get around to looking into purchasing insurance, the cost of care per month will be almost $9,800. Then, Mr. or Mrs. wise person (who just knew you were going to save money by waiting), they will ask something like this: Which do you think will cost more:

A. buying insurance to cover $6,000 per month at your current age based on your current health and at current rates, or

B. buying $9,800 per month of coverage (63% more) when you are 10 years older, probably in worse health and at the higher rates that the insurance company will very likely be charging at that time? Hello, is anybody home? They will go on to tell you that you have to understand that the insurance companies are not foolish. They are not pricing their policies in such a way as to encourage people to wait until they are old and decrepit before they purchase coverage. That wouldn't be very smart on their part, now would it? That is why thinking that if you wait until you are older to purchase coverage will result in saving money makes no sense whatsoever. They will also point out to those of you who are financial whizzes that even if you factor in the time value of money, you will still pay more by waiting until you are older.

So, be prepared because that is what they will tell you. I've seen 'em do it a million times. But don't worry, because as the old saying goes, "It will be too little too late." By then, it will be after the fact and either your health will be too far gone or the cost will be much greater than you will be willing to pay, so either way you win. So, don't be afraid that they will catch you at a weak moment and you will succumb to logic and reason. You will have time on your side and the time for taking action will have long since passed you by. Congratulations, you will have outsmarted them once again and by now almost nothing is left to stand in your way of *losing it all and ending up in a nursing home.*

All your friends will be there to shout "Bon voyage" as you leave them behind and set sail for the nursing home where your new life awaits.

Chapter 12
If I Never Need It, Then I Wasted My Money

I don't know who the genius was on our side who invented this one and started spreading it around, but I would sure like to meet them and personally congratulate them for all the good they have done to advance our cause. This one has absolutely caught on and spread like wildfire over the years and is single handedly responsible for untold numbers of people *losing it all and ending up in a nursing home.* He or she certainly deserves to be inducted into and hold a very prominent place in the Poverty Hall of Fame. The Poverty Hall of Fame is reserved for those people who, by all indications, had no business being there, but through the choices they made, they somehow ended up acquiring great poverty. If truth were told, the person who introduced this thought into the mainstream is largely responsible for rewriting the history of poverty in this country and creating a class called the "new poor." The "new poor" are those people who did not inherit poverty. They did not have the deck stacked against them from the start due to their environment, race, gender, education, family background, or anything else. From all appearances, you would never have expected them to climb down into the ranks of the poor. It wasn't easy and they had to go against everything they had ever been taught to pull it off. They pulled themselves down by their own bootstraps and accomplished it all on their own. Therefore, they are self-made and deserve all the credit for what they have accomplished.

You see, it used to be that poverty in this country was somewhat confined to the truly less fortunate who had so many obstacles stacked against them. Often times it was generational. If you ended up poor at the end of your life, it was because you had been poor all during your life. Not any more. All that has changed with the advances that have been made in the area of denialology, and poverty is now within the reach of almost anyone. This genius has made it possible for people of above average means to enjoy a very nice existence through the majority of their life and yet still be able to lose it all down the stretch. And that is exactly why this person, whoever they may be, is our hero and new best friend. They have contributed immensely to our goal of *losing it all and ending up in a nursing home*. For that, we all owe them a debt of gratitude. Let's start a petition to get a national holiday passed in their honor, what do you say?

Now, there is one little, teeny, tiny thing that someone from the other side (you know, the dark side) could possibly try to point out. I mean it's really, really small, really nothing at all, so forget that I even brought it up. Well, I can tell that you're not going to take "no" for an answer, so let me go ahead and get it over with. Just promise me that you will hear me out and stay with me until the end. Well, it all began back at the dawn of the information age when there was a movement started by a group of young truth reformers who challenged everything we believed and stood for. They did not care how much damage they caused to the progress we had made over many years. Fortunately, their message never really took hold because it was not an easy one to accept. It required people to actually accept responsibility for themselves and their families and to take action to protect themselves against bad things happening to them. Well, as you might imagine, that had about as much chance of becoming popular as people voluntarily signing up for root canals. However, there remains to this day a remnant of this group who have remained committed to this message and are relentless in doing whatever they can to keep people from *losing it all and ending up in a nursing home*. Because they are so small in number, you will rarely encounter them, but when you do, their modis operandi is very predictable. They will come at you with logic and reason and directly attack this little flaw that I was referring to in the belief that *if I never need it, then I wasted my money.*

They will say that you are basing whether you have received value by owning long-term care insurance on the wrong thing. And, by using the wrong standard to determine value, you are wrongly concluding that if you did not need to use it, then you wasted your money. They will point out that the true measure of the value of something varies from one category to another; therefore you must make sure that you are evaluating each category properly. For example, they would point out to you that the value of a bag of groceries has a different value than a rare piece of fine art and therefore, the value of both must be determined differently. Which one has the greater value? It depends on what your situation is at the precise moment. The groceries might have greater value if you were starving and without food, but if you had everything you needed, then the piece of fine art would probably be more valuable to you. If you were stranded on an island and help would not be there for another week, which would have the greatest value to you? And, even though the bag of groceries might have tremendous value to you today, if you set them in the corner and left them for a week and everything spoiled, how much value would they have then? So, they will try to get you to see that it is critical that you assess value based on the correct and proper criteria.

Here are a few of their favorite examples for illustrating their point. They will ask you: If a bank employs a security guard for 20 years and never has a robbery, did the bank waste their money by having the security guard? If a woman carries mace in her purse, but never has to use it, did she receive any value by having it? How many people judge the value they have received from the purchase of their alarm system in their home by how many times they have been burglarized? Isn't a big part of the value in all of these things that they prevent an undesirable event from occurring? Isn't another big part of the value the peace of mind and protection that they afford? How in the world can you put a price on that?

So, in other words, if you spend money to protect yourself from losing something that is important to you and you don't lose it, did you waste your money? They would say, "Of course not!" They would suggest that when a person owns long-term care insurance there is really no way they can lose. They reason that you win because of the peace of mind and protection you have even if the event never occurs, and you also win if the event does occur because you have minimized any loss that you would have suffered. So, either way, you win!

Well, if that isn't bad enough news for us, these zealots are relentless and they're not done yet. They really hit below the belt by having some of the most highly respected financial experts in the world weigh in on this issue. Few people are more respected in the financial world than Charles Schwab and Suze Orman. They will refer you to Charles Schwab's book entitled, *You're Fifty—Now What?* where he discusses long-term care insurance and says, "And if you buy it and never have to use it? Then consider yourself lucky, count your blessings, and know that you did the right thing by being prepared. You did the near impossible: You purchased peace of mind."[13] Then they will refer you to Suze Orman's book *9 Steps to Financial Freedom* where she says, "What if you never use long-term care insurance? It will be wonderful if that's the case. The purpose of insurance is to cover catastrophes. You should always hope you'll never have to use it."[14]

Well, you might think at this point that we're done. Toast! Ok, I admit that it is impossible to argue with their logic and that the best we can hope for is that it never comes up so we don't have to deal with it. But, the good news is, that is exactly what happens. Their message never gets out to the vast majority of our people. If it did, there is no question that our cause would suffer greatly. But, it's an unpopular message and not one our people want to hear. The only ones we are in jeopardy of losing are the few who really care about the truth, and you and I both know that while our people have been accused of a lot of things, accepting the truth if it conflicts with what they want to believe has never been one of them.

Chapter 13
I Talked to My (CPA, Attorney, Neighbor, Insurance Agent, etc.) and They Don't Think I Need It

I don't know if there is anything that is fool proof and works 100% of the time, but this one comes about as close as it gets. We all feel better when someone else tells us what we want to hear. If it's someone who we look up to and respect, then that's even better. It doesn't really matter what field they're in, we still take great comfort in their advice. It can be our CPA, attorney, neighbor, friend at work, insurance agent, or just about anyone. It lets us feel like we have done our research and homework, but share the responsibility for our decision with others, so it takes us off the hook a bit.

Everyone knows about the herd mentality: "there is safety in numbers" "everybody else is doing it" and, "the majority can't all be wrong." We find great comfort in doing what everyone else is doing, which is why that thing called peer pressure is so powerful. And, we aren't immune to it just because we become adults, it just takes on different forms. But, the bottom line is that it still causes our decisions to be influenced by what our peers are saying or doing.

Well, the good news is that we can use this powerful dynamic to our full advantage when it comes to advancing our cause of *losing it all and ending up in a nursing home.* In fact, this is nothing new because we have been using this one successfully for years and the old adage "if it ain't broke, don't fix it" certainly applies here. And, rest assured, we have every intention of continuing to exploit this one to the max. The cool thing is that we don't even have to convince people to do anything because this is something that they are already accustomed to doing. We just need to reinforce the behavior. They are already used to asking others for their opinions and advice about any and everything. Our ace in the hole is that since the vast majority of people are so misinformed about the subject of long-term care insurance, we already know the answer they will get, regardless of who they ask. It's completely predictable. It's almost as if the outcome is fixed. And it just so happens to be the answer that we want and need them to hear in order to advance our cause of making extreme poverty available to every man, woman, boy and girl regardless of race, gender, religion, or political affiliation. We believe that it is a basic human right and no one deserves to be left behind.

Well, no surprise here, the enemy has only one way to try and sabotage our mission. You guessed it, their weak, flimsy argument of logic and reason, and we already know how well that has worked for them in the past. Don't they get it that our people aren't interested? Read our lips, "We don't care." But, do you think that stops them? I don't think so! These people are absolutely relentless in their attempts to infiltrate our ranks and create doubt in the minds of our followers. Perhaps we should distribute a memo to the field letting them know the shrewd manner in which they are approaching our people. Their most recent attempts have centered on the following arguments. They begin by complimenting them and telling them how wise they are to research this issue, and how smart it is to seek advice from people they respect. But, it's at this point that they inject their logic and reason in order to create doubt and confusion. They will tell you that the problem is that most people talk to all of the *wrong* people and yet believe that they have done the *right* research. They will ask the following questions: Would you agree that research collected by talking to the wrong people or from the wrong sources is not going to help you make right decisions? Would you agree that you have to go to the right people in order to get the right information? If you have a legal matter, would you go to your CPA? If you have an accounting or tax question, would you go to your attorney? If your car is acting up, do you call the Maytag repairman? If you are dealing with emotional problems, do you see an orthopedic surgeon? If your computer crashes, do you call a plumber? Of course not! Any intelligent and reasonable person would certainly agree that this would make no sense at all. However, this is exactly what most people do when it comes to the area of long-term care insurance. They talk to all of the wrong people who give them all of the wrong answers. Why? Because the people who are being asked don't know any more about it, are just as misinformed, and are making the same mistakes as the people asking the questions. It's the classic case of the blind leading the blind.

Then, they will share true stories with you like the one individual who was quite concerned with this issue and therefore asked their well-respected financial advisor who had been in practice for over 20 years whether or not they should have long-term care insurance. He knew their situation quite well and told his client that they did not need to worry about it, and that they should be fine. Well, what's the problem? That sounds like reasonable advice. The financial advisor obviously felt that they had enough money that they could afford to self-insure, right? It is at this point that they will point out to you that this kind of thing happens all the time and go on to explain the following details. You see, perhaps this person really could afford to self-insure but did the financial advisor miss the part about whether that was something that they really *wanted* to do and that would have made them feel the most comfortable? The advisor had a huge clue staring them in the face— the client was concerned enough to bring the issue up in the first place. And, if they really could afford to self-insure, then the cost of the insurance, which would have been much less, would have been a non-issue, especially in exchange for the peace of mind that obviously was important to them. Next, you have to see if the financial advisor was consistent in his advice. Did he recommend cancelling all of their other types of insurance that were even less likely to be used than long-term care insurance and where the item being protected is of much less value? Obviously, this person could easily afford to self-insure those things. But, that isn't the incriminating part. That's just the part that falls into the "boy did he ever miss it" category.

They will remind you that this is a true story and this kind of thing happens all the time. They will continue by telling you that the worst part was that there was one other tiny, little detail that the financial advisor missed. This person already had cancer on not one, but two different occasions in very recent years. This was not someone who was the picture of health. In fact, almost every long-term care insurance company felt that the risk of this individual needing care in the future was so high that they would not touch it with a ten-foot pole. However, through much research, a top quality company was found that would have provided coverage. Now, if most of the best risk takers in the world—the insurance companies—didn't want to touch this one, and the client was already concerned enough about the issue to bring it up to the advisor, do you think the advisor gave them good advice in this area? Then they will finish making their case by referring you once again to Charles Schwab and Suze Orman for what they have to say on this particular matter.

Charles Schwab says, "It's easy to see that long-term care can wipe out an estate pretty quickly...Despite its newness, it's used more than any other kind of insurance–approximately one third of those who carry it end up using it." He goes on to say, "But this isn't solely a financial issue. There are other situations in which the peace of mind you get from having long-term care insurance may be more than worth the premiums."[15]

Suze Orman says, "As you will soon be able to tell, I love long-term care insurance. I believe that it's one of the most important policies you can have. Long-term care insurance is called into service more than any other kind."[16]

Well, there you have it. That is precisely the tact that they will take in trying to deceive you. They don't care about you. All they care about is squashing your dreams of *losing it all and ending up in a nursing home.* Now that you know how they will attack you in this area, you should be able to withstand and overcome their logic and reason with our weapons of denial and wishful thinking. You know the old saying, "To be forewarned is to be forearmed."

So, stand your ground, my friend, and it will be no time at all before you will be planting your flag in the fertile soil of the Shady Oaks atrium.

Chapter 14
The Premium Could Go Up in the Future

This is a simple, little one and more obscure than many of the others, but it can still be helpful in advancing our cause. The only problem with this one and the next belief in Chapter 15—*I may not be able to afford to keep it after I retire*—is that they are really last ditch efforts to just hang on for dear life. We know that when our people start reaching this far down into the bottom of the barrel, that they are becoming quite desperate for anything that will keep them from succumbing to the purchase of long-term care insurance. While their willingness to do almost anything to resist the enemy might seem like a good thing, in reality, it reveals that they are in a very tenuous position. It's as if they are in a free fall and are grasping for anything to hold onto on their way down.

When they have reached this point, we know that we are in serious jeopardy of losing them, so we will resort to anything. Now, we acknowledge that this argument is somewhat weak, but please bear with us, because it's about all we have left to work with. Okay, so here it is. Our strategy behind this one is to try and get them to worry about the premium increasing in the future (which may or may not ever happen) in order to keep their focus off the real issue. The second part of this strategy, and vital to its success, is to try and isolate this issue from every other area where they are used to increases in the cost of items such as food, electric, gasoline, taxes, cars, homes, etc. You want them to think that the possibility of this happening is a valid reason to avoid it altogether. Now, hopefully, you can do it so convincingly that their powers of denial will automatically kick in and cause their brain to shut down before they have a chance to figure out how illogical this is.

The problem is how easy it is for the other side to counteract this one. Our best defense is the hope that our follower's denial is so strong that they will put this issue to bed without giving the enemy an opportunity to respond. If they don't, then we are in grave trouble because the dark side will point out that almost everything in life increases in cost over time, and that certainly does not keep our followers from benefiting from each of the items listed above. They will also point out that long-term care insurance policies are priced with the intention of remaining level and not increasing over time. Therefore, should something happen and the companies ever need to adjust the premiums in the future, it would reveal that this problem was of even greater magnitude than the experts (the actuaries who study the data) predicted and would reinforce what a prudent decision they made by purchasing the insurance. The final thing they will do is to point out that almost all long-term care policies have a built-in feature called "waiver of premium" which means that once a person is on a claim and collecting benefits, they would no longer need to pay premiums. At that point, the premium would be irrelevant anyway.

Well, this is the best that we can do with one of our weaker beliefs. If this were the only belief we had to base our existence on, then we would be in serious trouble for sure. The good news, however, is that we have many other beliefs we can use to create layers and layers of impenetrable walls to keep the dark side at bay. With all of the tools we have provided, we are confident that you can find the way that works best for you to *lose it all and end up in a nursing home.* The power you need is entirely in your hands.

Chapter 15
I May Not Be Able to
Afford to Keep It After I Retire

This one is similar to its cousin, *the premiums could go up in the future.* It sounds somewhat reasonable on the surface, which is why we can include it in our repertoire. After all, everyone is concerned about retirement and whether or not they will have enough money to live comfortably, right? That is what makes this one seem so legitimate and plausible.

Now people, at this point I must pause and have a little heart to heart with you. Listen, we are all in this thing together trying to do everything we can to advance our cause of *losing it all and ending up in a nursing home,* right? Right. But, let's be honest, you and I both know that the arguments for supporting our beliefs come across as pretty weak and flimsy to the thinking person. Ok, granted we admit that, but that doesn't stop our cause from advancing because we have denial on our side and we know that denial when properly used can be more powerful than anything, including logic or reason. But, at the same time, we are trying to maintain some shred of dignity when it comes to how the outside world perceives us. And this is where many of you are blowing it and bringing much embarrassment to the cause. We do everything we can to provide you with the best beliefs and excuses possible for attaining our goals. And, we give you a vast array to choose from so that we have something for everyone, but with that comes a measure of responsibility on your part. I am getting reports back that many of our followers have no clue when it comes to the proper application of our beliefs. For example, I cannot tell you how many reports have crossed my desk of people who are combining belief number 8, *I'm just going to self-insure* with this one, *I may not be able to afford to keep it after I retire.*

Now folks, think about what you are saying. Heaven forbid, I'm not trying to bring the "L" word (logic) into this discussion, but you have got to pay attention and think about what you are doing. In the exact same interview with the other side many of you are saying that you have so much money that you can afford to self-insure this risk, but then in the next breath you're saying that you don't want to purchase the insurance because you don't know if you will be able to afford to pay the premiums after you retire. Hello, is anybody home? You can't have it both ways. Some of you guys are making us look ridiculous and there is absolutely no excuse for it. We provide so many resources to you in the form of published articles by so-called experts, chat rooms (your living room with friends and family), and professionals (attorneys, CPAs, financial advisors) who we have spent many years shaping their thinking and conditioning them to accept and promote our beliefs. Therefore, you are without excuse for not knowing how to properly apply our beliefs at your stage in the denial process. Now, please start paying more attention to what you are doing so that we can all make a positive contribution to how we are perceived by the outside world. I am sorry that I had to take that little diversion, but unfortunately, it was necessary and important.

Now, back to the belief at hand. Even though this one sounds legitimate because it ties into making sure we have enough money in retirement, it can also trip us up for the exact same reason. Have you ever made an excuse to someone to justify your reason for doing something, and as you were trying to get the words out realized that you didn't even believe it yourself, so you knew how it must be sounding to them? Or, as my friends in the South say, right in the middle of your explanation you realize "that dog don't hunt." You know what I'm talking about. You wish you hadn't even started down that path, but it's too late to turn back, so your voice starts trailing off and you kind of mumble near the end. Then, to add insult to injury, they ask, "I'm sorry, what did you say?" At that point, you feel like one of those people in the airline commercial who, after they have done something really embarrassing, the announcer comes on and says, "Want to get away?" Well, that is kind of what using this one is like. When you first say these words they make sense to you, but by the time you finish, even you are becoming aware of the inconsistency in what you are saying. You realize that if you are not sure you will be able to afford the premium in retirement, how would you ever be able to afford to pay for the much higher cost of the care itself? That is the risk in using this one and you need to be aware of it. It doesn't mean you can't still use it if you like, just be aware that if you are dealing with someone from the other side who is paying attention, they will call you on it and you could find it a little uncomfortable. Not to mention that you will have opened the door for them to share additional information that will be counter-productive to the cause. They will tell you that you should never spend more for long-term care insurance than you can comfortably afford, but also let you know that should something unforeseen happen and your situation change in the future, you can always adjust your coverage in order to lower your premium. They want you to be one of the few people who understand that you have this flexibility. Of course, they will also point out that if and when that were to happen, you could already be on a claim and using your policy, therefore you would not be paying premiums anyway. They will finish by encouraging you to make sure you don't take on the *certainty* of accepting this risk today to avoid the *uncertainty* of something that may never occur in the future.

Well, I guess we can't really blame them for trying. They are just doing what comes natural to them. You kind of have to admire their commitment to what they believe. And, you know what? They're really not bad people. In fact, truth be told, most of them are really quite likeable.

Well, anyway, let's all try and remember to be civil to them. We don't need any more PR fiascos than we've already been having lately.

Carry on!

Chapter 16
I'm Just Going to Shoot Myself

Now, although this one is not used as often as some of the others we have to choose from, many have used it regularly and effectively to accomplish our goal of *losing it all and ending up in a nursing home.* I know that some of you will be shocked by this one and cannot imagine how anyone could be so selfish and inconsiderate to ever say or think such a thing. I understand how you feel, but please don't shoot the messenger. Let's have some compassion on the poor souls who would choose to use this one. First off, you have to realize that it is usually us men who use this one. Do I need to say more? Okay, I admit that many of us are stubborn, a little self-centered, perhaps a tad insensitive, and frequently look for the easy way out, but other than that, we're really quite a catch. But, actually being that way is precisely what makes this one so effective in causing us to *lose it all and end up in a nursing home.* You women would never think to use this one, so we men are just trying to do our part, and since we're not quite as bright as you, this is the best that we can come up with.

Well, as much as I would like to try and be clever, this one calls for me to be serious with you for a moment, which is why I made this one our last belief.

Let me begin by saying that I have the utmost respect for you women and I think that you rarely get your due. It is my opinion that you are much more capable than us men. I personally believe that in general you are more organized, more capable of handling stress, better at juggling multiple tasks and responsibilities, and can handle pain much better than your knights in shining armor. It is so unfortunate that you are not appreciated more and taken for granted so much of the time. I can tell you for a fact that the business world would suffer greatly if it were not for what so many of you do to keep things going. Yeah, us men may be out front a lot of the time, but ask us if we would rather trade roles with you and try to handle everything you do. Does the term mass confusion mean anything to you?

I guess there is no better example of this than when it comes to this issue of long-term care. Once again, you women are the ones who this burden primarily falls on. Nothing bothers me more than when I meet with a couple and the woman is extremely concerned about this issue, but the husband (who many times makes the decisions) just doesn't care. He would rather go play golf, work on his boat, or do anything other than deal with this issue. Often times, no matter how concerned the wife is, the husband's vote carries the day and they end up doing nothing. It's no secret that statistically, the man is much more likely to need care first, and it will be the wife who will dutifully wait on her husband

and take care of him for perhaps many years. She will probably shoulder this burden alone, since often times the husband will not be willing to spend the money to provide her with any help or relief. Again folks, if he was not willing to spend the money on the insurance which is a fraction of the cost of actually paying for the care, do you really think he is going to step up to the plate and pay the much higher cost of the care when he can just have Mama do it? I don't think so! You know the 'ole saying "if Mama ain't happy, ain't nobody happy?" Well, you can kiss that saying goodbye! It's a new day. And a new day calls for a new way!

Not to mention that the effect that the stress of caregiving can have on the caregiver has been well documented. Studies have shown that frequently the caregivers own health is adversely affected and they even have a much higher death rate than non-caregivers.[17] Situations like this are occurring in homes across America every single day and you want to tell me that you can't see the value and difference that having long-term care insurance would make in these situations? I think we both know better than that.

Now, to you men who would say such a thing in order to avoid having to take responsibility for yourself and your families, let's have a little chat. One thing I will tell you is that I certainly admire your commitment to our program of *losing it all and ending up in a nursing home*, because what you are really saying is that you would be willing to die to make sure that this occurs. You don't realize it of course, but that is what you are saying. Here's why. You are using this excuse (shooting yourself) as a reason for not doing the very thing that could *keep you* from *losing it all and ending up in a nursing home.* The reality, as you will see in a minute, is that you will probably never follow through on your selfish threat. However, since it kept you from purchasing insurance to protect yourself and your family, your willingness to die is the very thing that will position you to *lose it all and end up in a nursing home.* Do you see it?

Now, let me tell you why you will probably never follow through on your plan. Actually, there are a whole host of reasons, so I will just list them for you:

First, I am giving you more credit for being a good husband and father and loving your family than you are giving yourself. No matter how selfish and inconsiderate you may be feeling right now, I honestly believe that in spite of whatever mistakes you may have made in the past, you will redeem yourself with one final act of love, consideration, and unselfishness. You may tell me that I am wrong, but I believe that there is hope for every person and I believe in you.

Secondly, if I am wrong, then I am going to go to the other extreme and bank on the fact that if you really are this self-centered, then the last thing you would want is to look bad to everyone who ever knew you. Would you really want your legacy (how you will be remembered) to be permanently marred by the way your life ended? Do you realize the emotional pain and trauma that you would be responsible for inflicting on your children and grandchildren? Are you aware that it is these types of tragedies that cause many people to turn to drugs and alcohol and change the entire course of their lives? Do you want to be responsible for that being the legacy you gave to your loved ones? Do you want their lasting memory of you to be a cowardly, selfish act that ruined their lives? Well if so, you will be pleased to know that your memory will be kept alive and well as you are discussed in their weekly therapy sessions for years to come.

Thirdly, what makes you think that you will even have the ability to plan and execute taking your own life when that time comes? What makes you think that you will even be able to remember that this was your plan in the first place? And exactly which loved one are you going to give the honor of being your accomplice? And are you okay with them going to jail for the rest of their lives for their part in your little plan? Oh, by the way, who's the lucky dog that gets to find you?

I could go on and on, but I think you get the point. Wouldn't it be an easier and better plan to just be a man and step up to the plate and care enough about your family (and yourself) to purchase long-term care insurance in order to give everyone a better quality of life? And, once you've done that and taken care of things, you can just forget about it and reward yourself by going to play golf or work on that boat of yours.

And, in my book *and* your family's, you'll definitely be The Man!

Chapter 17
So Where Do You Go From Here?

The price of this powerful little book was only $12.95, but if you're smart (and I'm betting you are) you will turn that small investment into one that saves you tens of thousands to hundreds of thousands of dollars. The choice is yours. You see, you may not have a lot of choice when it comes to the pills you need to take or the bills associated with your health care, but by now I hope you know that *losing it all and ending up in a nursing home* is optional and preventable for many people. I hope you have seen that instead of it being something that happens to us, it is usually something that we *do to ourselves*, but which is quite preventable.

Let me congratulate you for educating yourself. You may not realize it, but you are now more knowledgeable and informed about the real truth regarding the many myths that surround long term care insurance than 98% of the general public. And I am not just referring to the layperson; I am also talking about experts in other fields who opine about long-term care insurance—financial planners, CPAs, attorneys, authors, financial columnists, and even most insurance agents. I know because I work with almost all of these types of professionals and see how little they really know about this subject because it is not their field of expertise. The true professionals who are honest will admit it and refer you to a long-term care specialist. I know this also is true because I work with some of the smartest and best elder law attorneys, CPAs and financial planners in my area and they refer their clients to me for help in this very important area. They know and admit that it is not their field of expertise and care too much about their clients and their own reputation to jeopardize either.

Here is the next step I would encourage you to take immediately without procrastinating. If this book was given to you as a gift by an insurance professional or any type of financial advisor (CPA, attorney, financial planner, etc.), then I would contact the person or organization who gave you this book and tell them that you have read it and would like to talk to somebody about long-term care plans that might be right for your situation. The reason I suggest contacting them rather than someone else is because they thought enough of you and your financial well-being to make sure that you had access to the information contained in this book. It doesn't matter if you have used the same insurance agent for the last 30 years; if he or she has not had a serious discussion with you about long-term care insurance, then I certainly would not trust them to handle this issue for you. Sure, they will want to make a sale, so if you ask them about it, they will probably say that they can handle it for you. But, trust me; if they weren't the one to bring this to your attention, then they are not the person you would want to help you with this very important issue since they obviously do not specialize in this area. I would go so far as to say that even if they *have* mentioned long-term care insurance to you in the past, but were not able to demonstrate the importance of it well enough to cause you to take action to protect yourself, then they don't deserve your business now. Please don't misunderstand me here, I am not suggesting that you change any of the other insurance they handle for you, but I certainly would not trust them to handle something as specialized and important as this. What if something would have happened to you or if your health had changed before you received this information and decided to put a plan in place to protect yourself? Their life would not have been altered or skipped a beat, but yours could have dramatically changed.

Back to why I would contact the person or organization that gave you this book immediately and not delay. I know human nature and if you put it off, many things will come up that will keep you from ever addressing this issue. You are definitely to be commended for the knowledge that you now possess. However, if that knowledge does not result in your taking action to protect yourself and your family, then it is of no value to you. I would have wasted my time writing this book and you would have wasted your time reading it. If you have been enlightened and understand the truth about long-term care insurance and the importance of protecting yourself and your family, then whatever you do, please take action right now and do not procrastinate. You see, right at this moment you are in the best health that you will probably ever be in, are as young as you will ever be, and the rates for long-term care insurance are as low as they will ever be. Each one of these things is going to change and none of them for the better. Oh how I wish that you could hear the stories and phone calls I get from people who were going to protect themselves but never got around to it and now it's too late. Their health has changed and now they can't purchase long-term care insurance for all the money in the world. I can hear in their voices how upset and disappointed they are in themselves for procrastinating. All I can do is tell them how sorry I am and wish them well.

Please don't let that be your story. You really are without excuse now, because you know better. The vast majority of people do not have the knowledge that you have now acquired. I have given you my absolute best stuff in writing this book because I wanted to expose the myths that the whole world seems intent on believing when it comes to the subject of long-term care insurance.

Because of the tremendous denial around this issue, we have a major crisis in our country and with each passing day more and more people are *losing it all and ending up in nursing homes.* It's too late for them and they can never turn back the hands of time and do it over again. The sad thing is that if they could do it over again, you can bet they would do it differently. The only time to deal with this issue is in advance, *before* you find yourself in this situation. Don't buy into any of the lies and myths that have been exposed in this book even if everybody else around you chooses to believe them. Long-term care insurance is affordable; you can design the policy and cost to fit almost any budget. It is true that there are some people who really don't need long-term care insurance because they have so few assets and so little income that it would not make sense for them to purchase coverage. But, if you are reading this book, you are probably not in that category. In any event, don't make a decision as important as this on your own. Seek the advice and expertise of a qualified professional who will be more than happy to help you figure out whether long-term care insurance is right for you.

But, now that you are educated, don't keep it to yourself. Let's get the word out. Tell the people who you care about the most that they need to get *Pills and Bills* so they can learn the truth—the rest of the story—when it comes to long-term care insurance.

Many people and organizations have chosen to purchase this book in bulk quantities to share as a gift with their clients, friends, families, church groups, clubs, or other organizations. Both single copies and bulk quantities may be ordered at **www.PillsandBills.com**

Notes

[1] *Alzheimer's Disease Facts and Figures, 2007 study,* http://www.alz.org/ alzheimers_disease_facts_figures.asp.

[2] Houser, A.N., (2007). AARP Policy & Research. *Long-Term care Research Report,* http://www.aarp.org/research/longtermcare/trends/ fs27r_ltc.html.

[3] Friedland, R.B., (2004). Georgetown University Long-Term Care Financing Project. *Caregivers and long-term care needs in the 21st century: Will public policy meet the challenge?* http://ltc.georgetown. edu/pdfs/caregiversfriedland.pdf.

[4] Long Term Care Advisors, (2001). *Long Term Care is the Largest financial and emotional risk you and your family face today.* Submitted Testimony of the Honorable David F. Durenberger; Chairman, Citizens For Long Term Care to the United States Senate Special Committee on Aging, 6/28/01, http://www.ltcadvisor.info/sys/nl/ai.esp?cid=6260bce95f583 538e3ab9fa85dd94858&iid=4965&taf=0&show=11211&name=will %20you%20need%20long%20term%20care.

[5] Americans for Long-Term Care Security, (n.d.), http://www.ltcweb. org/More_than_half_of_the_US_population_will_require_long_ term_care_at_some_point_in_their_lives.cfm.

[6] Texas Department of Insurance, (n.d.), http://www.tdi.state.tx.us/ consumer/hicap/hicapltc05.html.

[7] AARP, (2005). *Beyond 50.2003: A Report to the Nation on Independent Living and Disability,* http://www.aarp.org/research/health/disabilities/ aresearch-import-753.html.

[8] Americans for Long Term Care Security, http://www.ltcweb.org/ Long_Term_Care.cfm.

[9] Tilly, J., O'Shaughnessy, C., Kelly, R., Sidov, G., Goldenson, S., Kasten, J., (2000) *Long-Term Care Chart Book: Persons Served, Payors, and Spending.* The Urban Institute, http://www.congress.gov/crsp/ lsd/00.122.doc.pdf.

[10] Report to Congress, Department of Health and Human Services' Office of the Assistant Secretary for Planning and Evaluation, (2003). *The Future Supply of Long-Term Care Workers in Relation to the Aging Baby Boom Generation,* http://aspe.hhs.gov/daltcp/reports/ltcwork.htm.

[11]Agency for Healthcare Research and Quality, (2000). *Long-term Care users range in age and most do not live in nursing homes*: Research alert. Rockville: Author, http://www.caregiver.org/caregiver/jsp/content_node. jsp?nodeid=440.

[12]Georgetown University Long-Term Care Financing Project Fact Sheet, (2003). *Who Needs Long Term Care?* http://ltc.georgetown.edu/ pdfs/whois.pdf.

[13]Schwab, C., (2001). *You're Fifty—Now What?* New York: Three Rivers Press.

[14]Orman, S., (1997). *9 Steps to Financial Freedom.* New York: Crown Publishers.

[15]Schwab, C., ibid.

[16]Orman, S., ibid.

[17]Planning for Eldercare, (2007). *Caregiving Stress – Hazardous to Your Health and Sometimes Deadly,* http://www.longtermcarelink.net/article-2007-12-11.htm.

To order single copies or bulk quantities of
Pills and Bills
to give to your clients, friends, families,
church groups, clubs, or other organizations go to
www.PillsandBills.com